How can this toolkit help you?

Buying a home is exciting and, let's face it, complicated. This booklet is a toolkit that can help you make better choices along your path to owning a home.

After you finish this toolkit:

How to use the toolkit:

The location symbol orients you to where you are in the home buying process.

The pencil tells you it is time to get out your pencil or pen to circle, check, or fill in numbers.

The magnifying glass highlights tips to help you research further to find important information.

The speech bubble shows you conversation starters for talking to others and gathering more facts.

About the CFPB

The Consumer Financial Protection Bureau is a federal agency that helps consumer finance markets work by making rules more effective, by consistently and fairly enforcing those rules, and by empowering consumers to take more control over their economic lives.

Have a question about a common consumer financial product or problem? You can find answers by visiting consumerfinance.gov/askcfpb. Have an issue with a mortgage, student loan, or other financial product or service? You can submit a complaint to the CFPB. We'll forward your complaint to the company and work to get you a response. Turn to the back cover for details on how to submit a complaint or call us at (855) 411-2372.

Choosing the best mortgage for you

 You're starting to look for a mortgage or want to confirm you made a good decision.

To make the most of your mortgage, you need to decide what works for you and then shop around to find it. In this section, you'll find eight steps to get the job done right.

1. Define what affordable means to you

Only you can decide how much you are comfortable paying for your housing each month. In most cases, your lender can consider only if you are able to repay your mortgage, not whether you will be comfortable repaying your loan. Based on your whole financial picture, think about whether you want to take on the mortgage payment plus the other costs of homeownership such as appliances, repairs, and maintenance.

 THE TALK

Ask your spouse, a loved one, or friend about what affordable means to you:

"What's more important—a bigger home with a larger mortgage or more financial flexibility?"

"How much do we want to budget for all the monthly housing costs, including repairs, furniture, and new appliances?"

"What will a mortgage payment mean for other financial goals?"

Think about what an affordable home loan looks like for you. These worksheets can help. First, estimate your total monthly home payment. Second, look at the percentage of your income that will go toward your monthly home payment. Third, look at how much money you will have available to spend on the rest of your monthly expenses.

Step 1. Estimate your total monthly home payment by adding up the items below

Your **total monthly home payment** is more than just your mortgage. There are more expenses that go along with owning your home. Start with estimates and adjust as you go.

	MONTHLY ESTIMATE
Principal and interest (P&I) Your principal and interest payment depends on your home loan amount, the interest rate, and the number of years it takes to repay the loan. **Principal** is the amount you pay each month to reduce the loan balance. **Interest** is the amount you pay each month to borrow money. Many principal and interest calculators are available online.	$
Mortgage insurance Mortgage insurance is often required for loans with less than a 20% down payment.	+ $
Property taxes The local assessor or auditor's office can help you estimate property taxes for your area. If you know the yearly amount, divide by 12 and write in the monthly amount.	+ $
Homeowner's insurance You can call one or more insurance agents to get an estimate for homes in your area. Ask if flood insurance is required.	+ $
Homeowner's association or condominium fees, if they apply Condominiums and other planned communities often require homeowner's association (HOA) fees.	+ $
My estimated total monthly home payment	= $

Step 2. Estimate the percentage of your income spent on your monthly home payment

Calculate the percentage of your total monthly income that goes toward your total monthly home payment each month. A mortgage lending rule of thumb is that **your total monthly home payment should be at or below 28% of your total monthly income before taxes.** Lenders may approve you for more or for less depending on your overall financial picture.

$$ \$ \underline{\hspace{3cm}} \div \$ \underline{\hspace{3cm}} \times 100 = \underline{\hspace{3cm}} \% $$

My estimated total monthly home payment (from step 1)   My total monthly income *before* taxes   Percentage of my income going toward my monthly home payment

Step 3. Estimate what is left after subtracting your monthly debts

To determine whether you are comfortable with your total monthly home payment, figure out how much of your income is left after you pay for your housing plus your other monthly debts.

Total monthly income *after* taxes	$
My estimated total monthly home payment (from step 1)	
Monthly car payment(s)	– $
Monthly student loan payment(s)	– $
Monthly credit card payment(s)	– $
Other monthly payments, such as child support or alimony	– $
Total monthly income minus all debt payments This money must cover your utilities, groceries, child care, health insurance, repairs, and everything else. If this isn't enough, consider options such as buying a less expensive home or paying down debts.	= $

Step 4. Your choice

I am comfortable with a total monthly home payment of: $ \underline{\hspace{4cm}}

2. Understand your credit

Your credit, your credit scores, and how wisely you shop for a loan that best fits your needs have a significant impact on your mortgage interest rate and the fees you pay. To improve your credit and your chances of getting a better mortgage, get current on your payments and stay current. About 35% of your credit scores are based on whether or not you pay your bills on time. About 30% of your credit scores are based on how much debt you owe. That's why you may want to consider paying down some of your debts.

🔍 RESEARCH STARTER

Check out interest rates and make sure you're getting the credit you've earned.

☐ Get your credit report at annualcreditreport.com and check it for errors. If you find mistakes, submit a request to each of the credit bureaus asking them to fix the mistake. For more information about correcting errors on your credit report, visit consumerfinance.gov/askcfpb.

☐ For more on home loans and credit, visit consumerfinance.gov/owning-a-home.

NOW

- If your credit score is below 700, you will likely pay more for your mortgage.

- Most credit scoring models are built so you can shop for a mortgage within a certain period—generally between 14 days and 45 days—with little or no impact on your score. If you shop outside of this period, any change triggered by shopping should be minor—a small price to pay for saving money on a mortgage loan.

IN THE FUTURE

- If you work on improving your credit and wait to buy a home, you will likely save money. Some people who improve their credit save $50 or $100 on a typical monthly mortgage payment.

- An average consumer who adopts healthy credit habits, such as paying bills on time and paying down credit cards, could see a credit score improvement in three months or more.

 YOUR CHOICE
Check one:

☐ I will go with the credit I have. OR ☐ I will wait a few months or more and work to improve my credit.

TIP

Be careful making any big purchases on credit before you close on your home. Even financing a new refrigerator could make it harder for you to get a mortgage.

TIP

Correcting errors on your credit report may raise your score in 30 days or less. It's a good idea to correct errors before you apply for a mortgage.

3. Pick the mortgage type—fixed or adjustable—that works for you

With a **fixed-rate mortgage**, your principal and interest payment stays the same for as long as you have your loan.

- Consider a fixed-rate mortgage if you want a predictable payment.

- You may be able to refinance later if interest rates fall or your credit or financial situation improves.

With an **adjustable-rate mortgage (ARM)**, your payment often starts out lower than with a fixed-rate loan, but your rate and payment could increase quickly. It is important to understand the trade-offs if you decide on an ARM.

- Your payment could increase a lot, often by hundreds of dollars a month.

- Make sure you are confident you know what your maximum payment could be and that you can afford it.

Planning to sell your home within a short period of time? That's one reason some people consider an ARM. But, you probably shouldn't count on being able to sell or refinance. Your financial situation could change. Home values may go down or interest rates may go up.

You can learn more about ARMs in the Consumer Handbook on Adjustable Rate Mortgages (files.consumerfinance.gov/f/201401_cfpb_booklet_charm.pdf) or by visiting consumerfinance.gov/owning-a-home.

YOUR CHOICE
Check one:

☐ I prefer a fixed-rate mortgage.   OR   ☐ I prefer an adjustable-rate mortgage.

Check for risky loan features

Some loans are safer and more predictable than others. It is a good idea to make sure you are comfortable with the risks you are taking on when you buy your home. You can find out if you have certain types of risky loan features from the Loan Terms section on the first page of your Loan Estimate.

A **balloon payment** is a large payment you must make, usually at the end of your loan repayment period. Depending on the terms of your loan, the balloon payment could be as large as the entire balance on your mortgage.

A **prepayment penalty** is an amount you have to pay if you refinance or pay off your loan early. A prepayment penalty may apply even if you sell your home.

> TIP
>
> Many borrowers with ARMs underestimate how much their interest rates can rise.

4. Choose the right down payment for you

A down payment is the amount you pay toward the home yourself. You put a percentage of the home's value down and borrow the rest through your mortgage loan.

 **YOUR CHOICE**
Check one:

YOUR DOWN PAYMENT	WHAT THAT MEANS FOR YOU
☐ I will put down 20% or more.	A 20% or higher down payment likely provides the best rates and most options. However, think twice if the down payment drains all your savings.
☐ I will put down between 5% and 19%.	You probably have to pay higher interest rates or fees. Lenders most likely require **private mortgage insurance (PMI)**. PMI is an insurance policy that lets you make a lower down payment by insuring the lender against loss if you fail to pay your mortgage.
	Keep in mind when you hear about "no PMI" offers that doesn't mean zero cost. No PMI offers often have higher interest rates and may also require you to take out a second mortgage. Be sure you understand the details.
☐ I will make no down payment or a small one of less than 5%.	Low down payment programs are typically more expensive because they may require mortgage insurance or a higher interest rate. Look closely at your total fees, interest rate, and monthly payment when comparing options.
	Ask about loan programs such as:
	• Conventional loans that may offer low down payment options.
	• FHA, which offers a 3.5% down payment program.
	• VA, which offers a zero down payment option for qualifying veterans.
	• USDA, which offers a similar zero down payment program for eligible borrowers in rural areas.

The advantages of prepayment

Prepayment is when you make additional mortgage payments so you pay down your mortgage early. This reduces your overall cost of borrowing, and you may be able to cancel your private mortgage insurance early and stop paying the premium. Especially if your down payment is less than 20%, it may make sense to make additional payments to pay down your loan earlier.

TIP

Prepayment is your choice. You don't have to sign up for a program or pay a fee to set it up.

5. Understand the trade-off between points and interest rate

Points are a percentage of a loan amount. For example, when a loan officer talks about one point on a $100,000 loan, the loan officer is talking about one percent of the loan, which equals $1,000. Lenders offer different interest rates on loans with different points. There are three main choices you can make about points. You can decide you don't want to pay or receive points at all. This is called a **zero point loan**. You can pay points at closing to receive a lower interest rate. Or you can choose to have points paid to you (also called **lender credits**) and use them to cover some of your closing costs.

The example below shows the trade-off between points as part of your closing costs and interest rates. In the example, you borrow $180,000 and qualify for a 30-year fixed-rate loan at an interest rate of 5.0% with zero points. Rates currently available may be different than what is shown in this example.

COMPARE THREE SCENARIOS OF HOW POINTS AFFECT INTEREST RATE

RATE	4.875%	5.0%	5.125%
POINTS	+0.375	0	-0.375
YOUR SITUATION	You plan to keep your mortgage for a long time. You can afford to pay more cash at closing.	You are satisfied with the market rate without points in either direction.	You don't want to pay a lot of cash upfront and you can afford a larger mortgage payment.
YOU MAY CHOOSE	Pay points now and get a lower interest rate. This will save you money over the long run.	Zero points.	Pay a higher interest rate and get a lender credit toward some or all of your closing costs.
WHAT THAT MEANS	You might agree to pay $675 more in closing costs, in exchange for a lower rate of 4.875%. **Now:** You **pay** $675 **Over the life of the loan:** Pay $14 **less** each month	With no adjustments in either direction, it is easier to understand what you're paying and to compare prices.	You might agree to a higher rate of 5.125%, in exchange for $675 toward your closing costs. **Now:** You **get** $675 **Over the life of the loan:** Pay $14 **more** each month

6. Shop with several lenders

You've figured out what affordable means for you. You've reviewed your credit and the kind of mortgage and down payment that best fits your situation. Now is the time to start shopping seriously for a loan. The work you do here could save you thousands of dollars over the life of your mortgage.

✎ GATHER FACTS AND COMPARE COSTS

☐ **Make a list of several lenders you will start with**
Mortgages are typically offered by community banks, credit unions, mortgage brokers, online lenders, and large banks. These lenders have loan officers you can talk to about your situation.

☐ **Get the facts from the lenders on your list**
Find out from the lenders what loan options they recommend for you, and the costs and benefits for each. For example, you might find a discount is offered for borrowers who have completed a home buyer education program.

☐ **Get at least three offers—in writing—so that you can compare them**
Review the decisions you made on pages 4 to 8 to determine the loan type, down payment, total monthly home payment and other features to shop for. Now ask at least three different lenders to give you a **Loan Estimate**, which is a standard form showing important facts about the loan. It should be sent to you within three days, and it shouldn't be expensive. Lenders can charge you only a small fee for getting your credit report—and some lenders provide the Loan Estimate without that fee.

☐ **Compare Total Loan Costs**
Review your Loan Estimates and compare Total Loan Costs, which you can see under *Section D* at the bottom left of the second page of the Loan Estimate. **Total Loan Costs** include what your lender charges to make the loan, as well as costs for services such as appraisal and title. The third page of the Loan Estimate shows the **Annual Percentage Rate** (APR), which is a measure of your costs over the loan term expressed as a rate. Also shown on the third page is the **Total Interest Percentage** (TIP), which is the total amount of interest that you pay over the loan term as a percentage of your loan amount. **You can use APR and TIP to compare loan offers.**

🔍 RESEARCH STARTER

Loan costs can vary widely from lender to lender, so this is one place where a little research may help you save a lot of money. Here's how:

☐ Ask real estate and title professionals about average costs in your area.

☐ Learn more about loan costs, and get help comparing options, at consumerfinance.gov/owning-a-home.

TIP

A loan officer is not necessarily shopping on your behalf or providing you with the best fit or lowest cost loan.

TIP

It is illegal for a lender to pay a loan officer more to steer you into a higher cost loan.

 **THE TALK**

Talking to different lenders helps you to know what options are available and to feel more in control. Here is one way to start the conversation:

"This mortgage is a big decision and I want to get it right. Another lender is offering me a different loan that may cost less. Let's talk about what the differences are and whether you may be able to offer me the best deal."

TRACK YOUR LOAN OFFERS
Fill in the blanks for these important factors:

	LOAN OFFER 1	LOAN OFFER 2	LOAN OFFER 3
Lender name			
Loan amount	$	$	$
Interest rate	%	%	%
	☐ Fixed ☐ Adjustable	☐ Fixed ☐ Adjustable	☐ Fixed ☐ Adjustable
Monthly principal and interest	$	$	$
Monthly mortgage insurance	$	$	$
Total Loan Costs *(See section D on the second page of your Loan Estimate.)*	$	$	$

My best loan offer is: _____

7. Choose your mortgage

You've done a lot of hard work to get this far! Now it is time to make your call.

Still need advice? The U.S. Department of Housing and Urban Development (HUD) sponsors housing counseling agencies throughout the country to provide free or low-cost advice. To find a HUD-approved housing counselor visit consumerfinance.gov/find-a-housing-counselor or call HUD's interactive voice system at (800) 569-4287.

Intent to proceed

When you receive a Loan Estimate, the lender has not yet approved or denied your loan. Up to this point, they are showing you what they expect to offer if you decide to move forward with your application. You have not committed to this lender. In fact, you are not committed to any lender before you have signed final closing documents.

Once you have found your best mortgage, the next step is to tell the loan officer you want to proceed with that mortgage application. This is called expressing your **intent to proceed**. Lenders have to wait until you express your intent to proceed before they require you to pay an application fee, appraisal fee, or most other fees.

Rate lock

Your Loan Estimate may show a rate that has been "locked" or a rate that is "floating," which means it can go up or down. Mortgage interest rates change daily, sometimes hourly. A **rate lock** sets your interest rate for a period of time. Rate locks are typically available for 30, 45, or 60 days, and sometimes longer.

The interest rate on your Loan Estimate is not a guarantee. If your rate is floating and it is later locked, your interest rate will be set at that later time. Also, if there are changes in your application—including your loan amount, credit score, or verified income—your rate and terms will probably change too. In those situations, the lender gives you a revised Loan Estimate.

There can be a downside to a rate lock. It may be expensive to extend if your transaction needs more time. And, a rate lock may lock you out of better market pricing if rates fall.

 THE TALK

Rate lock policies vary by lender. Choosing to lock or float your rate can make an important difference in your monthly payment. To avoid surprises, ask:

"What does it mean if I lock my rate today?"

"What rate lock time frame does this Loan Estimate provide?"

"Is a shorter or longer rate lock available, and at what cost?"

"What if my closing is delayed and the rate lock expires?"

"If I lock my rate, are there any conditions under which my rate could still change?"

8. Avoid pitfalls

WHAT NOT TO DO	WHY?
Don't sign documents where important details are left blank or documents you don't understand.	You are agreeing to repay a substantial amount of money over an extended period of time. Make sure you know what you are getting into and protect yourself from fraud.
Don't assume you are on your own.	HUD-approved housing counselors can help you navigate the process and find programs available to help first-time homebuyers. You can find a HUD-approved housing counselor in your area at consumerfinance.gov/find-a-housing-counselor or call HUD's interactive voice system at (800) 569-4287.
Don't take on more mortgage than you want or can afford.	Make certain that you want the loan that you are requesting and that you are in a position to live up to your end of the bargain.
Don't count on refinancing, and don't take out a loan if you already know you will have to change it later.	If you are not comfortable with the loan offered to you, ask your lender if there is another option that works for you. Keep looking until you find the right loan for your situation.
Don't fudge numbers or documents.	You are responsible for an accurate and truthful application. Be upfront about your situation. Mortgage fraud is a serious offense.
Don't hide important financial information.	Hiding negative information may delay or derail your loan application.

Handle problems

WHAT HAPPENED	WHAT TO DO ABOUT IT
I have experienced a problem with my loan application or how my loan officer is treating me.	Ask to talk to a supervisor. It may be a good idea to talk to the loan officer first, and if you are not satisfied, ask to speak with a supervisor.
I think I was unlawfully discriminated against when I applied for a loan or when I tried to buy a home.	The Fair Housing Act and Equal Credit Opportunity Act prohibit housing and credit discrimination. If you think you have been discriminated against during any part of the mortgage process, you can submit a complaint and describe what happened. To do so, you can call the Consumer Financial Protection Bureau at (855) 411-2372 or visit consumerfinance.gov/complaint. Submit a complaint to the U.S. Department of Housing and Urban Development (HUD) by calling (800) 669-9777, TTY (800) 927-9275. Or, file a complaint online at HUD.gov. You can find more information about your rights and how to submit a complaint with the CFPB at consumerfinance.gov/fair-lending.
I have a complaint.	Submit a complaint to the Consumer Financial Protection Bureau if you have problems at any stage of the mortgage application or closing process, or later if you have problems making payments or become unable to pay. You can call (855) 411-2372 or visit consumerfinance.gov/complaint.
I think I may have been the victim of a predatory lender or a loan fraud.	Don't believe anyone who tells you they are your "only chance to get a loan," or that you must "act fast." Learn the warning signs of predatory lending and protect yourself. Find more information at portal.hud.gov/hudportal/HUD?src=/program_ offices/housing/sfh/hcc/OHC_PREDLEND/OHC_LOANFRAUD. You could learn more about your loan officer at nmlsconsumeraccess.org.

Your closing

 You've chosen a mortgage. Now it's time to select and work with your closing agent.

Once you've applied for a mortgage, you may feel like you're done. But mortgages are complicated and you still have choices to make.

IN THIS SECTION

1. Shop for mortgage closing services

2. Review your revised Loan Estimate

3. Understand and use your Closing Disclosure

1. Shop for mortgage closing services

Once you've decided to move forward with a lender based on the Loan Estimate, you are ready to shop for the **closing agent** who gathers all the legal documents, closes the loan, and handles the money involved in your purchase. After you apply for a loan, your lender gives you a list of companies that provide closing services. You may want to use one of the companies on the list. Or, you may be able to choose companies that are not on the list if your lender agrees to work with your choice. The seller cannot require you to buy a title insurance policy from a particular title company.

TIP

Settlement services may feel like a drop in the bucket compared to the cost of the home. But in some states borrowers who shop around may save hundreds of dollars.

Closing agent

In most of the country, a settlement agent does your closing. In other states, particularly several states in the West, the person is known as an escrow agent. And in some states, particularly in the Northeast and South, an attorney may be required.

🔍 RESEARCH STARTER

When you compare closing agents, look at both cost and customer service.

☐ Ask your real estate professional and your friends. These people may know companies they would recommend. Be sure to ask how that company handled problems and if they have a good reputation.

☐ Review the list of companies your lender gave you. Select a few companies on the list and ask for references from people who recently bought a home. Ask those people how the company handled problems that came up during the transaction.

Title insurance

When you purchase your home, you receive a document most often called a deed, which shows the seller transferred their legal ownership, or "title," to the home to you. **Title insurance** can provide protection if someone later sues and says they have a claim against the home. Common claims come from a previous owner's failure to pay taxes or from contractors who say they were not paid for work done on the home before you purchased it.

Most lenders require a **Lender's Title Insurance** policy, which protects the amount they lent. You may want to buy an **Owner's Title Insurance** policy, which protects your financial investment in the home. The Loan Estimate you receive lists the Owner's Title Insurance policy as optional if your lender does not require the policy as a condition of the loan.

Depending on the state where you are buying your home, your title insurance company may give you an itemized list of fees at closing. This itemized list may be required under state law and may be different from what you see on your Loan Estimate or Closing Disclosure. That does not mean you are being charged more. If you add up all the title-related costs your title insurance company gives you, it should match the totals of all the title-related costs you see on your Loan Estimate or Closing Disclosure. When comparing costs for title insurance, make sure to compare the bottom line total.

Home inspector and home appraiser

When you are considering buying a home, it is smart to check it out carefully to see if it is in good condition. The person who does this for you is called a **home inspector**. The inspector works for you and should tell you whether the home you want to buy is in good condition and whether you are buying a "money pit" of expensive repairs. Get your inspection before you are finally committed to buy the home.

A home inspector is different from a **home appraiser**. The appraiser is an independent professional whose job is to give the lender an estimate of the home's market value. You are entitled to a copy of the appraisal prior to your closing. This allows you to see how the price you agreed to pay compares to similar and recent property sales in your area.

2. Review your revised Loan Estimate

When important information changes, your lender is required to give you a new Loan Estimate that shows your new loan offer.

It is illegal for a lender to quote you low fees and costs for its services on your Loan Estimate and then surprise you with much higher costs in a revised Loan Estimate or Closing Disclosure. However, a lender may change the fees it quotes you for its services if the facts on your application were wrong or changed, you asked for a change, your lender found you did not qualify for the original loan offer, or your Loan Estimate expired.

Here are common reasons why your Loan Estimate might change:

- You decided to change loan programs or the amount of your down payment.

- The appraisal on the home you want to buy came in higher or lower than expected.

- You took out a new loan or missed a payment and that has changed your credit.

- Your lender could not document your overtime, bonus, or other income.

THE TALK

If your Loan Estimate is revised you should look it over to see what changed. Ask your lender:

"Can you explain why I received a new Loan Estimate?"

"How is my loan transaction different from what I was originally expecting?"

"How does this change my loan amount, interest rate, monthly payment, cash to close, and other loan features?"

3. Understand and use your Closing Disclosure

You've chosen a home you want to buy and your offer has been accepted. You've also applied for and been approved for a mortgage. Now you are ready to take legal possession of the home and promise to repay your loan.

At least three days before your closing, you should get your official **Closing Disclosure**, which is a five-page document that gives you more details about your loan, its key terms, and how much you are paying in fees and other costs to get your mortgage and buy your home.

Many of the costs you pay at closing are set by the decisions you made when you were shopping for a mortgage. Charges shown under "services you can shop for" may increase at closing, but generally by no more than 10% of the costs listed on your final Loan Estimate.

The Closing Disclosure breaks down your closing costs into two big categories:

YOUR LOAN COSTS

- The lender's **Origination Costs** to make or "originate" the loan, along with application fees and fees to underwrite your loan. **Underwriting** is the lender's term for making sure your credit and financial information is accurate and you meet the lender's requirements for a loan.

- Discount points—that is, additional money you pay up front to reduce your interest rate.

- Services you shopped for, such as your closing or settlement agent and related title costs.

- Services your lender requires for your loan. These include appraisals and credit reports.

OTHER COSTS

- Property taxes.

- Homeowner's insurance premiums. You can shop around for homeowner's insurance from your current insurance company, or many others, until you find the combination of premium, coverage, and customer service that fits your situation. Your lender will ask you for proof you have an insurance policy on your new home.

- Any portion of your total mortgage payment you must make before your first full payment is due.

- Flood insurance, if required.

Q RESEARCH STARTER

Get tips, a step-by-step checklist, and help with the rest of the documents you'll see at closing at consumerfinance.gov/owning-a-home.

What is your Closing Disclosure?

The five-page Closing Disclosure sums up the terms of your loan and what you pay at closing. You can easily compare the numbers to the Loan Estimate you received earlier. There should not be any significant changes other than those you have already agreed to.

Take out your own Closing Disclosure, or review the example here. Double-check that you clearly understand what you'll be expected to pay—over the life of your loan and at closing.

ON PAGE 1 OF 5

Loan terms

Review your monthly payment. Part of it goes to repay what you borrowed (and may build equity in your new home), and part of it goes to pay interest (which doesn't build equity). Equity is the current market value of your home minus the amount you still owe on your mortgage.

Costs at Closing

Be prepared to bring the full "Cash to Close" amount with you to your closing. This amount includes your down payment and closing costs. The closing costs are itemized on the following pages.

Closing Disclosure

This form is a statement of final loan terms and closing costs. Compare this document with your Loan Estimate.

Closing Information

Date Issued	4/15/2013
Closing Date	4/15/2013
Disbursement Date	4/15/2013
Settlement Agent	Epsilon Title Co.
File #	12-3456
Property	456 Somewhere Ave
	Anytown, ST 12345
Sale Price	$180,000

Transaction Information

Borrower	Michael Jones and Mary Stone
	123 Anywhere Street
	Anytown, ST 12345
Seller	Steve Cole and Amy Doe
	321 Somewhere Drive
	Anytown, ST 12345
Lender	Ficus Bank

Loan Information

Loan Term	30 years
Purpose	Purchase
Product	Fixed Rate
Loan Type	☒ Conventional ☐ FHA ☐ VA ☐ _____
Loan ID #	123456789
MIC #	000654321

Loan Terms

		Can this amount increase after closing?
Loan Amount	$162,000	NO
Interest Rate	3.875%	NO
Monthly Principal & Interest *See Projected Payments below for your Estimated Total Monthly Payment*	$761.78	NO
		Does the loan have these features?
Prepayment Penalty	YES	• As high as $3,240 if you pay off the loan during the first 2 years
Balloon Payment	NO	

Projected Payments

Payment Calculation		Years 1-7		Years 8-30
Principal & Interest		$761.78		$761.78
Mortgage Insurance	+	82.35	+	—
Estimated Escrow *Amount can increase over time*	+	206.13	+	206.13
Estimated Total Monthly Payment		**$1,050.26**		**$967.91**

Estimated Taxes, Insurance & Assessments *Amount can increase over time* *See page 4 for details*	$356.13 a month	This estimate includes ☒ Property Taxes ☒ Homeowner's Insurance ☒ Other: Homeowner's Association Dues *See Escrow Account on page 4 for details. You must pay for other property costs separately.*	In escrow? YES YES NO

Costs at Closing

Closing Costs	$9,712.10	Includes $4,694.05 in Loan Costs + $5,018.05 in Other Costs – $0 in Lender Credits. *See page 2 for details.*
Cash to Close	$14,147.26	Includes Closing Costs. *See Calculating Cash to Close on page 3 for details.*

CLOSING DISCLOSURE   PAGE 1 OF 5 • LOAN ID # 123456789

Closing Disclosure, page 1. The most important facts about your loan are on the first page.

ON PAGE 2 OF 5

Total Loan Costs

Origination charges are fees your lender charges to make your loan. Some closing costs are fees paid to the providers selected by your lender. Some are fees you pay to providers you chose on your own.

Prepaids

Homeowner's insurance is often paid in advance for the first full year. Also, some taxes and other fees need to be paid in advance.

Closing Cost Details

Closing Cost Details

Loan Costs		Borrower-Paid		Seller-Paid		Paid by Others
		At Closing	Before Closing	At Closing	Before Closing	
A. Origination Charges		**$1,802.00**				
01 0.25 % of Loan Amount (Points)		$405.00				
02 Application Fee		$300.00				
03 Underwriting Fee		$1,097.00				
04						
05						
06						
07						
08						
B. Services Borrower Did Not Shop For		**$236.55**				
01 Appraisal Fee	to John Smith Appraisers Inc.					$405.00
02 Credit Report Fee	to Information Inc.		$29.80			
03 Flood Determination Fee	to Info Co.	$20.00				
04 Flood Monitoring Fee	to Info Co.	$31.75				
05 Tax Monitoring Fee	to Info Co.	$75.00				
06 Tax Status Research Fee	to Info Co.	$80.00				
07						
08						
09						
10						
C. Services Borrower Did Shop For		**$2,655.50**				
01 Pest Inspection Fee	to Pests Co.	$123.50				
02 Survey Fee	to Surveys Co.	$85.00				
03 Title – Insurance Binder	to Epsilon Title Co.	$650.00				
04 Title – Lender's Title Insurance	to Epsilon Title Co.	$500.00				
05 Title – Settlement Agent Fee	to Epsilon Title Co.	$500.00				
06 Title – Title Search	to Epsilon Title Co.	$800.00				
07						
08						
D. TOTAL LOAN COSTS (Borrower-Paid)		**$4,694.05**				
Loan Costs Subtotals (A + B + C)		$4,664.25	$29.80			

Other Costs

Other Costs		Borrower-Paid		Seller-Paid		Paid by Others
		At Closing	Before Closing	At Closing	Before Closing	
E. Taxes and Other Government Fees		**$85.00**				
01 Recording Fees	Deed: $40.00 Mortgage: $45.00	$85.00				
02 Transfer Tax	to Any State			$950.00		
F. Prepaids		**$2,120.80**				
01 Homeowner's Insurance Premium (12 mo.) to Insurance Co.		$1,209.96				
02 Mortgage Insurance Premium (mo.)						
03 Prepaid Interest ($17.44 per day from 4/15/13 to 5/1/13)		$279.04				
04 Property Taxes (6 mo.) to Any County USA		$631.80				
05						
G. Initial Escrow Payment at Closing		**$412.25**				
01 Homeowner's Insurance $100.83 per month for 2 mo.		$201.66				
02 Mortgage Insurance per month for mo.						
03 Property Taxes $105.30 per month for 2 mo.		$210.60				
04						
05						
06						
07						
08 Aggregate Adjustment		– 0.01				
H. Other		**$2,400.00**				
01 HOA Capital Contribution	to HOA Acre Inc.	$500.00				
02 HOA Processing Fee	to HOA Acre Inc.	$150.00				
03 Home Inspection Fee	to Engineers Inc.	$750.00			$750.00	
04 Home Warranty Fee	to XYZ Warranty Inc.			$450.00		
05 Real Estate Commission	to Alpha Real Estate Broker			$5,700.00		
06 Real Estate Commission	to Omega Real Estate Broker			$5,700.00		
07 Title – Owner's Title Insurance (optional) to Epsilon Title Co.		$1,000.00				
08						
I. TOTAL OTHER COSTS (Borrower-Paid)		**$5,018.05**				
Other Costs Subtotals (E + F + G + H)		$5,018.05				
J. TOTAL CLOSING COSTS (Borrower-Paid)		**$9,712.10**				
Closing Costs Subtotals (D + I)		$9,682.30	$29.80	$12,800.00	$750.00	$405.00
Lender Credits						

CLOSING DISCLOSURE

Details of your closing costs appear on page 2 of the Closing Disclosure.

Escrow

An escrow or impound account is a special account where monthly insurance and tax payments are held until they are paid out each year. You get a statement showing how much money your lender or mortgage servicer plans to require for your escrow or impound account.

You also get an annual analysis showing what happened to the money in your account. Your lender must follow federal rules to make sure they do not end up with a large surplus or shortage in your escrow or impound account.

USE YOUR CLOSING DISCLOSURE TO CONFIRM THE DETAILS OF YOUR LOAN

Circle one. If you answer no, turn to the page indicated for more information:

The interest rate is what I was expecting based on my Loan Estimate.   YES / NO (see page 10)

I know whether I have a prepayment penalty or balloon payment.   YES / NO (see page 7)

I know whether or not my payment changes in future years.   YES / NO (see page 7)

I see whether I am paying points or receiving points at closing.   YES / NO (see page 9)

I know whether I have an escrow account.   YES / NO (see above)

Calculating Cash to Close

Closing costs are only a part of the total cash you need to bring to closing.

Summaries of Transactions

The section at the bottom of the page sums up how the money flows among you, the lender, and the seller.

Loan Disclosures

Page 4 breaks down what is and is not included in your escrow or impound account. Make sure you understand what is paid from your escrow account and what you are responsible for paying yourself.

Top image: A summary of important financial information appears on page 3 of the Closing Disclosure.

Bottom image: More details of your loan appear on page 4 of your Closing Disclosure.

Calculating Cash to Close

Use this table to see what has changed from your Loan Estimate.

	Loan Estimate	Final	Did this change?
Total Closing Costs (J)	$8,054.00	$9,712.10	YES • See Total Loan Costs (D) and Total Other Costs (I)
Closing Costs Paid Before Closing	$0	– $29.80	YES • You paid these Closing Costs before closing
Closing Costs Financed (Paid from your Loan Amount)	$0	$0	NO
Down Payment/Funds from Borrower	$18,000.00	$18,000.00	NO
Deposit	– $10,000.00	– $10,000.00	NO
Funds for Borrower	$0	$0	NO
Seller Credits	$0	– $2,500.00	YES • See Seller Credits in Section L
Adjustments and Other Credits	$0	– $1,035.04	YES • See details in Sections K and L
Cash to Close	$16,054.00	$14,147.26	

Summaries of Transactions

Use this table to see a summary of your transaction.

BORROWER'S TRANSACTION

K. Due from Borrower at Closing	$189,762.30
01 Sale Price of Property	$180,000.00
02 Sale Price of Any Personal Property Included in Sale	
03 Closing Costs Paid at Closing (J)	$9,682.30
04	
Adjustments	
05	
06	
07	

Adjustments for Items Paid by Seller in Advance

08 City/Town Taxes	to	
09 County Taxes	to	
10 Assessments	to	
11 HOA Dues	4/15/13 to 4/30/13	$80.00
12		
13		
14		
15		

L. Paid Already by or on Behalf of Borrower at Closing	$175,615.04
01 Deposit	$10,000.00
02 Loan Amount	$162,000.00
03 Existing Loan(s) Assumed or Taken Subject to	
04	
05 Seller Credit	$2,500.00

SELLER'S TRANSACTION

M. Due to Seller at Closing	$180,080.00
01 Sale Price of Property	$180,000.00
02 Sale Price of Any Personal Property Included in Sale	
03	
04	
05	
06	
07	
08	

Adjustments for Items Paid by Seller in Advance

09 City/Town Taxes	to	
10 County Taxes	to	
11 Assessments	to	
12 HOA Dues	4/15/13 to 4/30/13	$80.00
13		
14		
15		
16		

N. Due from Seller at Closing	$115,665.04
01 Excess Deposit	
02 Closing Costs Paid at Closing (J)	$12,800.00
03 Existing Loan(s) Assumed or Taken Subject to	
04 Payoff of First Mortgage Loan	$100,000.00
05 Payoff of Second Mortgage Loan	

Additional Information About This Loan

Loan Disclosures

Assumption

If you sell or transfer this property to another person, your lender
☐ will allow, under certain conditions, this person to assume this loan on the original terms.
☒ will not allow assumption of this loan on the original terms.

Demand Feature

Your loan
☐ has a demand feature, which permits your lender to require early repayment of the loan. You should review your note for details.
☒ does not have a demand feature.

Late Payment

If your payment is more than 15 days late, your lender will charge a late fee of 5% of the monthly principal and interest payment.

Negative Amortization (Increase in Loan Amount)

Under your loan terms, you
☐ are scheduled to make monthly payments that do not pay all of the interest due that month. As a result, your loan amount will increase (negatively amortize), and your loan amount will likely become larger than your original loan amount. Increases in your loan amount lower the equity you have in this property.
☐ may have monthly payments that do not pay all of the interest due that month. If you do, your loan amount will increase (negatively amortize), and, as a result, your loan amount may become larger than your original loan amount. Increases in your loan amount lower the equity you have in this property.
☒ do not have a negative amortization feature.

Partial Payments

Your lender
☒ may accept payments that are less than the full amount due (partial payments) and apply them to your loan.
☐ may hold them in a separate account until you pay the rest of the payment, and then apply the full payment to your loan.
☐ does not accept any partial payments.
If this loan is sold, your new lender may have a different policy.

Security Interest

You are granting a security interest in
456 Somewhere Ave., Anytown, ST 12345

You may lose this property if you do not make your payments or satisfy other obligations for this loan.

Escrow Account

For now, your loan
☒ will have an escrow account (also called an "impound" or "trust" account) to pay the property costs listed below. Without an escrow account, you would pay them directly, possibly in one or two large payments a year. Your lender may be liable for penalties and interest for failing to make a payment.

Escrow		
Escrowed Property Costs over Year 1	$2,473.56	Estimated total amount over year 1 for your escrowed property costs: *Homeowner's Insurance Property Taxes*
Non-Escrowed Property Costs over Year 1	$1,800.00	Estimated total amount over year 1 for your non-escrowed property costs: *Homeowner's Association Dues* You may have other property costs.
Initial Escrow Payment	$412.25	A cushion for the escrow account you pay at closing. See Section G on page 2.
Monthly Escrow Payment	$206.13	The amount included in your total monthly payment.

☐ will not have an escrow account because ☐ you declined it ☐ your lender does not offer one. You must directly pay your property costs, such as taxes and homeowner's insurance. Contact your lender to ask if your loan can have an escrow account.

No Escrow	
Estimated Property Costs over Year 1	Estimated total amount over year 1. You must pay these costs directly, possibly in one or two large payments a year.
Escrow Waiver Fee	

In the future,

Your property costs may change and, as a result, your escrow payment may change. You may be able to cancel your escrow account, but if you do, you must pay your property costs directly. If you fail to pay your property taxes, your state or local government may (1) impose fines and penalties or (2) place a tax lien on this property. If you fail to pay any of your property costs, your lender may (1) add the amounts to your loan balance, (2) add an escrow account to your loan, or (3) require you to pay for property insurance that the lender buys on your behalf, which likely would cost more and provide fewer benefits than what you could buy on your own.

Loan Calculations

Total of Payments. Total you will have paid after you make all payments of principal, interest, mortgage insurance, and loan costs, as scheduled.	$285,803.36
Finance Charge. The dollar amount the loan will cost you.	$118,830.27
Amount Financed. The loan amount available after paying your upfront finance charge.	$162,000.00
Annual Percentage Rate (APR). Your costs over the loan term expressed as a rate. This is not your interest rate.	4.174%
Total Interest Percentage (TIP). The total amount of interest that you will pay over the loan term as a percentage of your loan amount.	69.46%

Questions? If you have questions about the loan terms or costs on this form, use the contact information below. To get more information or make a complaint, contact the Consumer Financial Protection Bureau at www.consumerfinance.gov/mortgage-closing

Other Disclosures

Appraisal
If the property was appraised for your loan, your lender is required to give you a copy at no additional cost at least 3 days before closing. If you have not yet received it, please contact your lender at the information listed below.

Contract Details
See your note and security instrument for information about
• what happens if you fail to make your payments,
• what is a default on the loan,
• situations in which your lender can require early repayment of the loan, and
• the rules for making payments before they are due.

Liability after Foreclosure
If your lender forecloses on this property and the foreclosure does not cover the amount of unpaid balance on this loan,
☒ state law may protect you from liability for the unpaid balance. If you refinance or take on any additional debt on this property, you may lose this protection and have to pay any debt remaining even after foreclosure. You may want to consult a lawyer for more information.
☐ state law does not protect you from liability for the unpaid balance.

Refinance
Refinancing this loan will depend on your future financial situation, the property value, and market conditions. You may not be able to refinance this loan.

Tax Deductions
If you borrow more than this property is worth, the interest on the loan amount above this property's fair market value is not deductible from your federal income taxes. You should consult a tax adviser for more information.

Contact Information

	Lender	Mortgage Broker	Real Estate Broker (B)	Real Estate Broker (S)	Settlement Agent
Name	Ficus Bank		Omega Real Estate Broker Inc.	Alpha Real Estate Broker Co.	Epsilon Title Co.
Address	4321 Random Blvd. Somecity, ST 12340		789 Local Lane Sometown, ST 12345	987 Suburb Ct. Someplace, ST 12340	123 Commerce Pl. Somecity, ST 12344
NMLS ID					
ST License ID			Z765416	Z61456	Z61616
Contact	Joe Smith		Samuel Green	Joseph Cain	Sarah Arnold
Contact NMLS ID	12345				
Contact ST License ID			P16415	P51461	PT1234
Email	joesmith@ ficusbank.com		sam@omegare.biz	joe@alphare.biz	sarah@ epsilontitle.com
Phone	123-456-7890		123-555-1717	321-555-7171	987-555-4321

Confirm Receipt

By signing, you are only confirming that you have received this form. You do not have to accept this loan because you have signed or received this form.

Applicant Signature	Date	Co-Applicant Signature	Date

CLOSING DISCLOSURE

PAGE 5 OF 5 • LOAN ID# 123456789

Loan calculations, disclosures, and contact information for your files are on page 5 of the Closing Disclosure.

Finance Charge

In addition to paying back the amount you are borrowing, you pay a lot of interest over the life of the loan. This is why it is worthwhile to shop carefully for the best loan for your situation.

Annual Percentage Rate (APR)

Your **APR** is your total cost of credit stated as a rate. Your APR is generally higher than your interest rate, because the APR takes into consideration all the costs of your loan, over the full term of the loan.

If anything on the Closing Disclosure is not clear to you, ask your lender or settlement agent, "What does this mean?"

NOW

- Now you've spent time understanding what you need to do and what you need to pay, as a new homeowner.

- Now is the time to step back and feel sure you want to proceed with the loan.

IN THE FUTURE

- If you are not comfortable with your mortgage and your responsibility to make payments, you might not be able to keep your home.

- If you've made a careful decision about what you can afford and the mortgage you wanted, you will be able to balance owning your home and meeting your other financial goals.

Owning your home

 Now you've closed on your mortgage and the home is yours.

Owning a home is exciting. And your home is also a large investment. Here's how to protect that investment.

1. Act fast if you get behind on your payments

If you fall behind on your mortgage, the company that accepts payments on your mortgage contacts you. This company is your **mortgage servicer**. Your servicer is required to let you know what options are available to avoid foreclosure. Talk to your mortgage servicer if you get into trouble, and call a housing counselor (see page 12 for contact information). HUD-approved counselors are professionals who can help you, often at little or no charge to you.

Homeowners struggling to pay a mortgage should beware of scammers promising to lower mortgage payments. Only your mortgage servicer can evaluate you for a loan modification. If you suspect a scam you can call (855) 411-2372 or visit consumerfinance.gov/complaint.

2. Keep up with ongoing costs

Your mortgage payment is just one part of what it costs to live in your new home. Your escrow account holds your monthly taxes and homeowner's insurance payments—but if you have no escrow account, you need to keep up with these on your own. Your home needs maintenance and repairs, so budget and save for these too.

3. Determine if you need flood insurance

Flooding causes more than $8 billion in damages in the United States in an average year. You can protect your home and its contents from flood damage. Depending on your property location, your home is considered either at high-risk or at moderate-to-low risk for a flood. Your insurance premium varies accordingly. You can find out more about flood insurance at FloodSmart.gov. Private flood insurance could also be available.

Although you may not be required to maintain flood insurance on all structures, you may still wish to do so, and your mortgage lender may still require you to do so to protect the collateral securing the mortgage. If you choose to not maintain flood insurance on a structure, and it floods, you are responsible for all flood losses relating to that structure.

4. Understand Home Equity Lines of Credit (HELOCs) and refinancing

Homeowners sometimes decide they want to borrow against the value of their home to help remodel or pay for other large expenses. One way to do this is with a **Home Equity Line of Credit** (HELOC). You can learn more about HELOCs at files.consumerfinance.gov/f/201401_cfpb_booklet_heloc.pdf.

Financial counselors caution homeowners against using a HELOC to wipe out credit card debt. If you use a HELOC as a quick fix to a serious spending problem, you could end up back in debt and lose your home.

If you decide to take out a HELOC or refinance your mortgage, the Truth in Lending Act (TILA) gives you the **right to rescind**, meaning you can change your mind and cancel the loan. But you can only rescind a refinance or HELOC within three days of receiving a proper notice of the right to rescind from your lender. You cannot rescind if you are using your HELOC to buy a home.

In the case of a refinance, consider how long it will take for the monthly savings to pay for the cost of the refinance. Review the closing costs you paid for your original loan to purchase the home. Refinancing costs can be about the same amount. A common rule of thumb is to proceed only if the new interest rate saves you that amount over about two years (in other words, if you break even in about two years).

★ Congratulations!

You have accomplished a lot. It is not easy—you should feel proud of the work you've done.